A TRUE BOOK W9-AYD-213

Cesar Chavez

JOSH GREGORY

Children's Press®
An Imprint of Scholastic Inc.
New York Toronto London Auckland Sydney
Mexico City New Delhi Hong Kong
Danbury, Connecticut

Content Consultant
James Marten, PhD
Professor and Chair, History Department
Marquette University
Milwaukee, Wisconsin

Library of Congress Cataloging-in-Publication Data
Cesar Chavez / Josh Gregory.
     pages cm. — (A true book)
  Includes bibliographical references and index.
  ISBN 978-0-531-21172-4 (library binding) — ISBN 978-0-531-21210-3 (pbk.)
1. Chavez, Cesar, 1927–1993—Juvenile literature. 2. Labor leaders—United States—Biography—
Juvenile literature. 3. Mexican American migrant agricultural laborers—Biography—Juvenile
literature. 4. United Farm Workers—History—Juvenile literature. 5. Migrant agricultural laborers—
Labor unions—United States—History—Juvenile literature. I. Title.
  HD6509.C48G74 2015
  331.88'13092—dc23[B]   2014032317

Scholastic Inc., 557 Broadway, New York, NY 10012.

Front cover: Chavez at a rally

**Back cover: Chavez working
at a community garden**

Find the Truth!

Everything you are about to read is true *except* for one of the sentences on this page.

Which one is **TRUE**?

T or F Cesar Chavez spent two years in the U.S. Navy.

T or F Cesar Chavez led a strike against apple growers in 1965.

Find the answers in this book.

3

Contents

4

Cesar Chavez led striking farm workers on a protest march in 1966.

4 An Ongoing Battle

How did Chavez keep fighting for workers' rights after the grape strike ended? **35**

Cesar Chavez led a nationwide boycott of grapes to raise awareness for farm workers' rights.

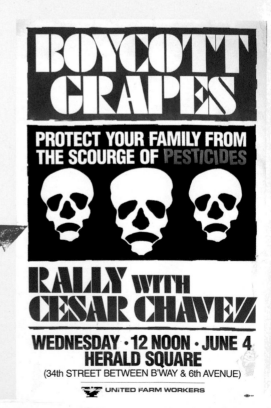

BOYCOTT GRAPES

PROTECT YOUR FAMILY FROM THE SCOURGE OF PESTICIDES

RALLY WITH CESAR CHAVEZ

WEDNESDAY · 12 NOON · JUNE 4
HERALD SQUARE
(34th STREET BETWEEN B'WAY & 6th AVENUE)

UNITED FARM WORKERS

5

Cesar Chavez changed farm
labor in the United States.

CHAPTER 1

Humble Beginnings

Farmworkers play an important role in the way we live. Without their hard work, we would not see such a variety of fresh produce at our local grocery stores. Even though these men and women perform backbreaking labor to provide millions of people with food, their employers have treated them very poorly throughout history. In the 1960s, one farmworker decided to do something about this unfair treatment. His name was Cesar Chavez.

← Cesar Chavez's birthday is celebrated as a holiday in several states.

The American Dream

Cesar's grandparents, Cesario and Dorotea Chavez, moved to the United States from Mexico in the 1880s. They settled near Yuma, Arizona, and began farming the land. They had been poor in Mexico, but they soon found success with their new life in the United States. Their children, including a son named Librado, helped them work the farm.

The land around Yuma still supports successful farms today.

Cesar Chavez was named after his grandfather, Cesario.

➡️

Tough Times

On March 31, 1927, Librado's wife, Juana, gave birth to a baby boy. The proud parents named their son Cesar. Cesar had a happy childhood at first. He had a warm, loving family. However, the 1930s were a tough time for many Americans. The Great Depression ruined the nation's **economy**, and **drought** struck much of the country. As a result, the Chavez family was forced to give up their farm.

A part of a farmworker's wages was often based on how much he or she picked.

Cesar's family moved to San Jose, California, where they lived in a garage in a poor neighborhood. To earn money, they worked on other people's farms. Cesar and his family picked everything from peas and grapes to beans and avocados. This was hard work, and they were paid very little. A California farmworker in the early 1940s might make less than 50 cents an hour, a fraction of what other workers earned.

From the Classroom to the Field

Cesar split his time between farmwork and school. Different crops are harvested at different times of the year. As seasons changed, the Chavez family often traveled to pick these crops. This meant that Cesar attended many different schools. By the time he finished eighth grade, he decided to quit school altogether to work full-time in the fields. He wanted to earn more money so his mother wouldn't have to work.

Cesar and his siblings pose with the family's car.

11

Lessons Learned

Even though Cesar stopped going to school, he never stopped learning. He loved to read, and he educated himself about subjects such as history and politics in his spare time. He was especially interested in the stories of political **activists** such

as Mahatma Gandhi. Gandhi used peaceful protests to free the people of India from British rule.

Mahatma Gandhi's actions, speeches, and writings inspired many people, both in India and around the world.

Cesar called his time in the navy "the two worst years of [his] life."

Love and War

In 1943, Cesar met Helen Fabela at a malt shop. The teenagers had a lot in common. Like the Chavezes, Helen's family members were **migrant** and seasonal farmworkers. In 1946, Cesar joined the U.S. Navy and traveled to Asia, keeping in touch with Helen back home. However, Cesar quickly decided that military life was not right for him. He returned home in 1948. Soon after, he married Helen and settled down to start a family.

Chavez and Fred Ross worked together for many years.

CHAPTER 2

A New Direction

In 1952, a man named Fred Ross arrived in San Jose. Ross was part of a group called the Community Service Organization (CSO). The CSO worked to help poor people and **immigrants** who had legally moved to the United States to make a fresh start and earn U.S. citizenship. The organization helped them find homes, jobs, and access to legal services and medical care. The CSO was also an activist group that fought against unfair treatment by companies and government organizations.

← Fred Ross founded the CSO in the late 1940s.

Cesar Chavez (front row, far right) and his wife, Helen (back row, third from right), both worked with the CSO.

Rising in the Ranks

Ross had come to San Jose to start a local CSO branch. He met with farmworkers and other people throughout the area who might be interested in joining the group. Chavez decided to become involved. He began traveling across the region, where he met with countless migrant and seasonal farmworkers. He talked to them about the importance of workers' rights and encouraged them to vote in elections.

The Bracero Program

When the United States entered World War II (1939–1945) late in 1941, many of the people who owned or worked on farms traveled overseas to fight. To make sure farms kept producing crops, the U.S. government began a new program in 1942. It allowed Mexican workers, called braceros, to legally and temporarily work in the United States. Braceros worked for less money than many Americans. After the war ended, growers were unwilling to give up this inexpensive labor, and the program continued.

As he visited farms and talked to workers during much of the 1950s, Chavez recognized a major problem with the way growers ran their businesses. Many of them relied heavily on braceros to provide cheap field labor. This helped the growers keep wages very low, even for the American citizens they hired. It also made it difficult for many American farmworkers to find jobs at all.

Priest and activist Father Thomas McCullough talks with a family about their living and working conditions as migrant farmworkers.

Farm workers often worked as part of a large group in the fields.

Going Public

As he went about his CSO duties, Chavez learned more about the ways growers abused the bracero program. He helped organize a **strike** for workers to protest the use of braceros and the low wages they were paid. These actions helped call widespread attention to the growers' misuse of the bracero program.

The reputation Chavez built as a strong, outspoken leader during his work with the CSO stuck with him the rest of his life.

A Small Victory

Thanks in part to Chavez's work, the bracero program came under heavy criticism from much of the nation. This would eventually lead to the program's end in 1964. In the meantime, however, Chavez had more work to do. Having seen his remarkable ability to lead and inspire people, CSO leaders chose him to be the new national director of the organization.

Bigger Goals

Chavez began to think of new ways he could improve the lives of migrant and seasonal farmworkers. He determined that one of the best ways to do this would be to help them form a powerful **union**. Workers in other industries had used unions to win better pay, improved working conditions, and much more. If they could do it, Chavez reasoned, then so could farmworkers.

Throughout the 20th century, many different workers, including garment workers, had used unions to obtain better treatment.

21

Farms employed workers of all ages, often using the labor of entire families.

CHAPTER 3

United Against Oppression

Chavez saw firsthand the many struggles that farmworkers faced on a regular basis. There were often no bathrooms for the workers to use. Drinking water was usually not provided, even though picking crops was hot, hard work. Conditions were unsafe, and many workers died in accidents. Some growers even put children to work in their fields. Chavez believed that creating a union could help solve these problems.

Laws against child labor are not as strict for farm jobs.

Leaving CSO

The other leaders of the CSO knew that forming such a union would be risky and difficult. They decided that they would rather continue operating as they had before. As a result, Chavez left to form his own organization in 1962. Calling it the National Farm Workers Association (NFWA), Chavez began traveling throughout California in search of supporters, just as he had for the CSO years earlier.

Dolores Huerta (second from left) and Chavez (far right) both played important roles in the NFWA.

The black eagle is based on Mexican and Aztec imagery.

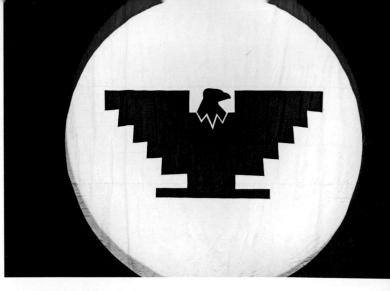

The NFWA logo later became the United Farm Workers logo.

A Slow Start

Building the union went slowly at first. However, Chavez was determined. He met face-to-face with migrant and seasonal workers across the state and soon built a solid network of supporters. In spring 1965, he led the union's first strike. Eighty-five workers on a rose farm refused to work until the growers raised their wages. After several days, the growers gave in. The NFWA had won its first victory, but it was only the beginning.

Grape pickers faced strenuous work for little pay.

Agricultural Allies

Around the same time, members of a similar group called the Agricultural Workers Organizing Committee (AWOC) staged a strike of their own. Their strike took place among grape pickers in California's Coachella Valley. Like the NFWA, they were able to win a wage increase after a few days of refusing to work. Afterward, the strike ended, and the AWOC members went back to work.

The Strike Begins

After the harvest in the Coachella Valley, many of the same workers moved on to harvest grapes near the town of Delano. There, they expected the same increased wages they had won earlier. However, the growers refused to pay. Once again, the AWOC began a strike. This time, the AWOC asked Chavez to help. Because the NFWA was a very large group, the strike expanded quickly. By fall 1965, thousands of workers were refusing to pick grapes.

Most members of the NFWA were Mexican American. The AWOC members were mainly Filipino.

Chavez leads strikers and supporters during the strike in Delano.

27

Peaceful Protest

The strike continued into 1966. Chavez led the striking workers using the tactics of peaceful activists such as Gandhi and civil rights leader Martin Luther King Jr. Chavez believed that peaceful protests such as strikes and **pickets** were the most effective way to make a difference. With this in mind, groups of workers took part in demonstrations across thousands of acres of grape fields. They gathered in different places each day.

Martin Luther King Jr. helped lead peaceful marches and other demonstrations during the 1950s and 1960s to support civil rights for African Americans.

Men on tractors drive by strikers, creating thick, choking dust clouds.

Standing Strong

The growers fought back against the strikers. First, they tried to hire non-NFWA and -AWOC workers to replace them. However, members of the picketing organizations often convinced these workers to join the strike. As growers became more desperate, their allies in local police departments began harassing strikers and even arresting them, often on false charges. Chavez encouraged the workers to stand strong and remain peaceful. He knew that fighting back violently would hurt their reputation.

Chavez talks with striking workers in a worker's home.

Not Enough

Soon, growers attempted to end the strike by offering to match the wages paid by the Coachella Valley growers. However, this small success had encouraged the workers to keep fighting. They would no longer be satisfied with wage increases alone. Instead, they began demanding that the growers officially recognize the NFWA and the AWOC as unions.

Official recognition would grant the NFWA and the AWOC far more power to defend their members against unfair treatment from growers. Instead of striking, the unions would have the legal right to bargain with employers and demand reasonable pay and working conditions. Growers did not want their workers to have such power. As a result, they decided to continue fighting the strike.

Chavez and his followers continued the strike, demanding widespread, longer-lasting changes.

A Nation of Supporters

Chavez and other members of the NFWA and the AWOC traveled the country giving speeches about farmworkers' rights. They also launched a **boycott** of grapes grown by companies that refused to deal with the striking organizations. As a result, people other than farmworkers also participated in the protest against California's grape growers.

Student activists, church groups, and other protesters all joined the cause. They stopped buying grapes and encouraged other people to do the same. They even visited grocery stores to tell the customers why the boycott was important.

By the end of the 1960s, millions of people throughout the United States and Canada were boycotting California grapes and wines. As a result, grape sales fell drastically, putting major pressure on California's growers to negotiate with strike organizers.

CHAPTER 4

An Ongoing Battle

In March 1966, Chavez and 70 strikers began marching from Delano to Sacramento, California's state capital. Their route would lead them about 340 miles (547 kilometers) on foot. The marchers carried signs and banners so observers would know why they were marching. Along the way, hundreds more people joined them. News reporters and camera crews soon heard about the march, and brought it to national attention.

The march to Sacramento began on March 17, 1966.

Signs of Success

As the marchers gained attention from across the country and the boycott caused grape sales to drop, some of California's biggest grape growers began to worry. One of the biggest, Schenley Industries, realized that it was no use fighting the strike any longer. They began negotiating an agreement with NFWA leaders.

Chavez developed severe blisters during the march. He had to walk with a cane.

A crowd of people gathered at the capitol building in Sacramento to hear Chavez speak.

The marchers arrived in Sacramento 25 days after leaving Delano. By this time, the march had swelled to include thousands of people. In front of the state capitol, Chavez happily delivered good news to the marchers: Schenley had signed documents agreeing to recognize the NFWA as a union. In August, the AWOC officially joined the NFWA to form a single organization, with Chavez as its leader. This union became the United Farm Workers Association (UFW).

The Next Steps

Even though Schenley had recognized the union, the strike was far from over. The region was home to many grape growers. Most of them still refused to give in. Chavez encouraged the striking workers to be patient and stick to peaceful protests. By 1968, however, some of the workers did not think change was happening fast enough. They wanted to return to work and earn money, and they were willing to use violence to get their way.

Timeline of Chavez's Activism

1962

Chavez founds the National Farm Workers Association and begins gathering members.

1965

The NFWA joins the AWOC grape pickers' strike.

Going Hungry

Chavez knew he needed to make a big statement to show the workers the power of peaceful resistance. In February 1968, he began a **fast**. For 25 days, he did not eat anything and drank only water. Through his quiet protest, Chavez succeeded once again in drawing widespread attention to the cause. At the end of the fast, New York senator Robert F. Kennedy came to California to share bread with Chavez.

1970
All grape growers agree to recognize the UFW as a union.

1968
Chavez goes on a 25-day fast in support of nonviolent resistance.

1966
The NFWA and the AWOC merge to form the United Farm Workers.

Twenty-six growers signed a contract with the UFW on July 29, 1970.

Victory at Last

In 1970, five years after the strike began, victory was finally at hand. That year, the region's grape growers all agreed to accept the UFW as an official union. About 50,000 workers would now receive health care, better pay, and improved working conditions. In addition, union representatives could ensure that the growers did not **discriminate** when hiring workers. It had been a long and difficult battle, but it had finally paid off.

Chavez's Final Fast

Farmworkers continued to face many challenges. In 1988, Chavez began a final fast. He hoped to call attention to the dangerous pesticides (chemicals used to kill insects) used by some growers. After 36 days, Chavez became too weak to continue the fast. Some of Chavez's famous friends, such as Jesse Jackson, Edward James Olmos, and Whoopi Goldberg, continued the fast in his place. Such dedication and support brought the issue national attention, though change did not take place during Chavez's lifetime.

BOYCOTT GRAPES

PROTECT YOUR FAMILY FROM THE SCOURGE OF PESTICIDES

RALLY WITH CESAR CHAVEZ

WEDNESDAY · 12 NOON · JUNE 4
HERALD SQUARE
(34th STREET BETWEEN B'WAY & 6th AVENUE)

UNITED FARM WORKERS

Later Efforts

The grape strike of the 1960s would remain Chavez's greatest victory. Still, he continued to fight for workers' rights for the rest of his life. The UFW helped organize workers in several states outside of California. Chavez also worked with politicians to pass laws giving unions and farmworkers more rights.

The UFW began using the motto "¡Sí, se puede!" (meaning, roughly, "Yes, we can!") in 1972.

Chavez led a massive strike and boycott campaign in the 1970s to support lettuce pickers.

About 35,000 people attended Chavez's funeral.

Not Forgotten

In 1993, Chavez died peacefully in his sleep at his home in San Luis, near Yuma, Arizona, not far from the farm where he had been born. When his funeral was held in Delano, thousands of people came to pay their respects. Today, he is still remembered by workers everywhere as they struggle to continue the fight for fair treatment. ★

Number of people gathered at the end of Chavez's 1966 march from Delano to Sacramento: About 10,000

Length of the march from Delano to Sacramento: About 340 miles (547 km)

Number of days it took the marchers to reach Sacramento: 25

Number of supporters of the national grape boycott: About 17 million

Number of times Chavez fasted: 3

Time Chavez went without eating during his 1968 fast: 25 days

Length of Chavez's longest fast: 36 days

Did you find the truth?

T Cesar Chavez spent two years in the U.S. Navy.

F Cesar Chavez led a strike against apple growers in 1965.

Resources

Books

Hile, Kevin. *Cesar Chavez: UFW Labor Leader*. Detroit: Lucent Books, 2008.

Warren, Sarah. *Dolores Huerta: A Hero to Migrant Workers*. New York: Marshall Cavendish Children, 2012.

Visit this Scholastic Web site for more information on Cesar Chavez:
★ www.factsfornow.scholastic.com
Enter the keywords **Cesar Chavez**

Important Words

activists (AK-tiv-ists) — people who work for some kind of social change

boycott (BOI-kaht) — a refusal to buy something or do business with someone as a punishment or protest

discriminate (dis-CRIM-uh-nate) — to treat some people better than others for an unfair reason

drought (DROUT) — a long period without rain

economy (i-KAH-nuh-mee) — the system of buying, selling, making things, and managing money in a place

fast (FAST) — the practice of eating no food for a period of time

immigrants (IM-i-gruhnts) — people who move from one country to another and settle there

migrant (MYE-gruhnt) — a person who moves from one area or country to another

pickets (PIK-its) — acts of standing outside a place in protest

strike (STRIKE) — a refusal to go to work until an employer meets certain demands

union (YOON-yuhn) — an organized group of workers set up to help improve such things as working conditions, wages, and health benefits

Index

Page numbers in **bold** indicate illustrations.

About the Author

Josh Gregory writes and edits books for kids. He lives in Chicago, Illinois.